Enter the

Poems

by

Jay Appleton

Jay Appleton

With Illustrations by

Geoffrey Shovelton

Shov

The Wildhern Press 2009

Published by

The Wildhern Press

131 High St.
Teddington
Middlesex TW11 8HH

Copyright Jay Appleton 2009

www.echo-library.com

ISBN 978-1-84830-207-5

AMY AND THE FAIRIES

Amy was of that noble breed
  Who thrive on doing good.
She'd put out bits of cake to feed
  The fairies in the wood.

And when she visited the scene
  After the break of day,
She'd find the fairy folk had been
  And cleared them all away.

The members of her family
  Were sceptical enough.
They said it was the milkman; he
  Was knocking off the stuff!

But Amy wasn't having it.
  'The *fairies* took the food,
'Carried the goodies bit by bit
  'To eat them in the wood!'

Amy, determined she would win
  And prove her story right,
Went off to find the fairies in
  The middle of the night.

She had to pinch herself to see
   She really was awake,
But there they were voraciously
   Consuming bits of cake!

A witch with cunning artifice
   To Amy's great surprise
Had turned them into fairy mice
   Three times the normal size.

'And that', said she, 'is how I know
   'We've fairies, gnomes and elves,
'And if you don't believe me, go
   'And see them for yourselves'.

But Daddy had a better thought
   And with a knowing grin
Took Amy to the shop and bought
   Some fairy Warfarin.

A drop to
wash it
down?

BADGER'S WOOD

When as a child I went to Badger's Wood
I looked for all the characters I knew,
Little Miss Muffet and Red Riding hood,
Little Bo-peep and Humpty Dumpty too.
And though I never saw them in the flesh
I always felt their presence in the air.
Each time I went I searched for them afresh
Because I simply *knew* that they were there.
We leave these childish fantasies behind
But curiosity can still contrive
To rouse a sense of wonder in the mind
And keep the mood of mystery alive.
My grandson tells me Rupert Bear was seen
Furtively snogging with the Fairy Queen.

BAGHDAD REGATTA

Some politicians emulate
The stalwart men of rowing.
Like oarsmen in a racing eight
They can't see where they're going!

THE BALLAD OF HALTEMPRICE AND HOWDEN

(On 12th June 2008, The Rt Hon David Davis, Conservative M.P. for the Haltemprice and Howden Constituency and Shadow Home Secretary, resigned his seat at Westminster in order to force a by-election in which he intended 'to provoke a wider public debate on the single issue of the perceived erosion of civil liberties'. The events which followed are set out hereunder).

'My name is David Davis and I have a tale to tell:
'This lousy Labour Government is out to give us hell.
'George Orwell's awful prophecy in *Nineteen Eighty-Four*
'Is now a stark reality. We can't take any more!
'A comprehensive database, as anyone can see,
'Will menacingly take away our fragile privacy.
'The camera will watch us from the cradle to the grave

'And woe-betide the citizen who dares to misbehave!
'Twenty-eight days in custody they think are far too few,
'So now the bastards want to put it up to forty-two,
'While other gross impertinences, even worse than these,
'Foreshadow the erosion of our civil liberties.

9

'Why should we meekly suffer when the going's getting tough?
'We persecuted citizens have more than had enough.
'It simply isn't good enough to turn the other cheek;
'Now is the providential hour for Haltemprice to speak!
'In protest at the Nanny State I now resign my seat.
'My Membership of Parliament is finally complete.
'Roll on the by-election, then!   Fall in and follow me!
'We'll show these would-be despots what we think of tyranny!
'Stand up for civil liberties.   Be resolute and bold.
'Forget I said it was a job I didn't want to hold.
'Whether you generally vote Conservative or not,
'Elect me to the office which I had already got!'
Thus angrily the Member for the seat of Haltemprice
Lacking the calming benefit of Cameron's advice,
Proceeded to initiate a series of events
Which powerfully managed to eclipse all precedents.
With Liberal Democracy predictably inclined
To sympathise with principles which Davis had in mind,
And Labour, in a hesitant and pessimistic mood,
Aware another drubbing wouldn't do them any good,
Neither would field a candidate to fly their party flag,
So Davis now predictably had got it in the bag!
The drama quickly gathered pace and very soon we find
All sorts of crackpot candidates, each with an axe to grind,
Are sucked into the vacuum and enter the debate
Among the dumb-struck members of a stunned electorate.
A more unlikely gathering one scarcely could conceive;
The drivel we were treated to you never would believe.
So David Davis won the seat and unconvincingly
Claimed, as he obviously would, a stunning victory!
What, then, has been the consequence of his bizarre crusade

And does he think he's justified the protest he has made?
We residents of Haltemprice will not be taken in;
The argument for what he did is wearing pretty thin.
His well-intentioned exercise brazenly claimed to be
A final referendum on our threatened liberty.
It threw up some statistics, as all referenda do,
Confirming independently what we already knew.
It cost a lot of money too.   Why yes, of course it did!
A widely rumoured estimate was eighty thousand quid,
Which is a pretty handsome price to pay for marshalling
A pack of so-called evidence that didn't prove a thing!
In fairness, give him credit for his noble sacrifice;
In sticking to his principles he's had to pay a price;
His glowing future prospects have received a heavy blow
And all he has achieved is to restore the *status quo*.
By way of consolation I'll admit it's rather nice
To think that lots of people now have heard of Haltemprice.
With six and twenty candidates contending for the prize
Prospects of notoriety appear before our eyes.
The Guinness Book of Records now is on the likely list
Of golden opportunities which surely can't be missed!
The proper course of action, then, is plain enough to see;
We need new legislation to recover sanity,
Requiring that a Member who relinquishes a seat
Before their ordinary term of office is complete
Should have to do the decent thing; forfeit the right to stand
In the resulting by-election they themselves had planned.
And meanwhile let us not abuse elections any more
By using them for purposes they're not in tended for.

THE CHASING GAME

Jessica, Robert and Nicholas Paul,
They rush through the kitchen and into the hall.
They rush like a whirlwind, they go like a gale
With everyone chasing another one's tail.
They charge down the passage and into the loo;
They rush through the lounge and the dining-room too.
Mummy says 'Careful!' and 'Mind you don't fall,
'Jessica, Robert and Nicholas Paul!'

Jessica, Robert and Nicholas Paul,
Rushing around like a tropical squall!
They rush up the stairs and they rush down again;
They rush through the house like a runaway train,
Rushing around at a frightening pace,
Chasing each other all over the place.
That's how we love to remember them all,
Jessica, Robert and Nicholas Paul!

CHEMISTRY

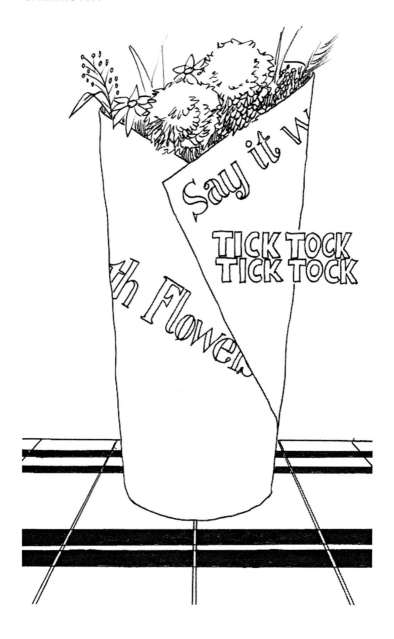

When Alistair and Annabel announced their wedding day
My dear old Auntie Agatha was overheard to say
'What admirable news!   It's what I've prayed for every night;
'They're made for one another, dear.   The chemistry is right!'

Now why, I ask, 'the chemistry'?   A curious word to choose!
An unromantic image for a bridal pair to use.
It conjures up a picture of a test tube or a pill;
There must be other sciences that better fit the bill!

The language of the botanist would be a better bet
With phrases like 'forget-me-not' or 'rose' or 'mignonette'.
'Love-in-the-mist' or 'lavender' or 'Venus' looking-glass'
Would seem a better prospect than a canister of gas.

Or what of ornithology?   The sentimental dove
Is surely more convincing than 'the chemistry of love'.
But if we're after Venus and we're looking for a clue
Perhaps the astrophysicists would know a thing or two.

For eighteen months or thereabouts the marriage limped along,
But sadly, dear Aunt Agatha, the chemistry was *wrong*!
It proved to be shambolic, if you'll overlook my slang.
Like all that's best in chemistry it finished with a bang!

CLASS DISTINCTION

Sir Randolph Campbell-Fortescue
Was rabidly committed to
Those standards which we now forget,
Good manners, style and etiquette;
So every letter he addressed
Had got to pass this stringent test:
'Did it accord the addressee
'His status in society?'
He'd not approach a baroness
As if she were a governess
Or take the liberty to write
'Mister' when writing to a knight.
These principles he staunchly kept
But one exception he'd accept:
The cost of postage stamps should be
The same throughout society,
One scale of charges be applied
To all our letters countrywide.
A duke, a marquis or a tramp
Paid the same money for a stamp.
When 'First' and 'Second' started he
Was challenged by a quandary:
A 'Second' is all right, and yet
Not for a knight or baronet
For fear they'd think he saw them as
Only deserving 'Second Class',
Placing them in his hierarchy
Lower than where they ought to be.

Yet why, he asked himself, should he
Placate the aristocracy
By forking out the extra dough?
And that is what he'd like to know!
Therefore, no matter what their rank,
Title or balance in the Bank,
He just refused to play the game
And treated everyone the same.
Furious to find his style was cramped,
He sent out everything unstamped,
And, though the principle appealed
To have a level playing-field,
If Randolph Campbell-Fortescue
Should condescend to write to you,
In consequence of what he did
You'll pay the postage - *plus a quid*!

CONFESSIONAL

Among the sins we should confess
You'll find the sin of idleness.
It's mild enough when placed beside
A proper sin like homicide.
It's better, though, that we eschewed
All trace of moral turpitude,
Insisting that we always try
To keep our moral standards high,
And so I've struggled to repress
What was described as 'laziness'.
The lazy habit, it appears,
Grows stronger with advancing years
Thus threatening in many ways
The golden sunset of our days,
But now it has belatedly
Achieved respectability.
The symptoms may be just the same
But now they have a Latin name!

THE CONVERSION OF FARMER BLIGH

When Farmer Bligh went harvesting in Nineteen-twenty-three
The rural English scenery was as it ought to be;
The fields were gleaming golden and the hedges gleaming green
Which made the most enchanting sight that you had ever seen.
The horses pulled the binder and the binder cut the corn
While half the village rallied round to hail the smiling morn.
To celebrate the Harvest-home they roasted half a sheep
And drank themselves delirious before they went to sleep.

*

When Farmer Bligh went harvesting in Nineteen-eighty-five
All sorts of things had happened since his Grandad was alive.
He'd been to university and learnt a thing or two;
He'd little good to say about the things they *used* to do.
But, having sacked the workers who had been in his employ,
He wasn't very popular among the *hoi polloi*;

They didn't like his attitude; they didn't like his style;
They thought his haughty arrogance was positively vile.
They didn't like the ostentatious cars he used to run
While grumbling that a farmer's lot is not a happy one.
They didn't like the batteries in which he housed his hens;
They said he kept his bullocks in unsanitary pens.
They wouldn't have it that his hens were salmonella-free
And neither would they eat his beef because of BSE.
They didn't like the nitrates that he used to boost his yields;
They didn't like the way he shut the footpaths through his fields.
They didn't like the way he sprayed his pesticides about;
It nearly caused a riot when he grubbed his hedges out.
And when in Nineteen-eighty-five the harvesting was done,
Before they went to Benidorm to find a spot of sun,
They held their Harvest Supper in the kitchen at The Hall,
Just Farmer Bligh and Mrs Bligh and no-one else at all.
Instead of roasting half a sheep, as Grandad would have done,
With bitter by the barrelful and cider by the tun,
They satisfied their hunger with a Chinese takeaway
And washed it down with Foster's on a television tray.

*

A formidable lady came and called on Farmer Bligh.
A rabid conservationist, she made the feathers fly!
She bullied him, she badgered him she drove him up the wall
And radically changed the situation at The Hall.
He joined the Greens and lots of other pressure-groups besides;
He unequivocally damned the use of herbicides,
While artificial fertilisers simply wouldn't do
And anabolic steroids were decidedly taboo.
He breathed the word 'organic' with a deferential awe,
Appraising ecologically everything he saw.
'My Fordson and my Ferguson will have to go!' he said;
'I'll buy a team of Percherons to do the job instead.'

He planted pretty coppices for everyone to see;
He dedicated rights of way in perpetuity,
And if he saw a fellow-farmer burning off the straw
He wouldn't hesitate to call the forces of the law.
He re-instated hedges and he re-engaged his men;
Within their graves his ancestors slept peacefully again.

*

So when it came to harvest time in Nineteen-ninety-four
The scene was as idyllic as it ever was before.
The workers and their families, invited to The Hall
To celebrate the Harvest-home responded to the call.
Once more around the festive board foregathered all the folk.
There wasn't anything to eat 'cos Farmer Bligh was broke!

DICING WITH DEATH

You try my patience, wretched little fly,
Tickling annoyingly my arm and hand.
I know you have to, and the reason why
Is something I can fully understand.
I have a theory that you seem to like
My skin when lightly seasoned by my sweat.
Though I've attempted many a well-aimed strike
I've not been quick enough to catch you yet.
'Old man, your theory's no more accurate
'Than your attempts to do me lethal harm.
'Haven't you noticed how I choose to wait
'Till the last moment on your hairy arm?
'Nothing to do with your disgusting skin!
'I get my kicks from my adrenalin!'

EIGHTY-EIGHT

I always hoped I'd get to eighty-eight
Before I got the call to go to Hades,
And now I've made it I can hardly wait
To meet those legendary Two Fat Ladies!

AN ESSAY ON MAN

'*The proper study of Mankind is Man*'.
You mean that 'Woman' is an also-ran?
If so you force me, Alexander Pope,
To write you off as a deluded dope,
For if I have to study him or her
She is the one I'd very much prefer.
Shame on your chauvinistic prejudice!
You don't know what you're asking us to miss!
Away with this implied misogyny!
You keep the boys but leave the girls to me!
What's that you say? You're misinterpreted?
Thank God! I thought you must be off your head!

THE ETHICAL OWL

The owl that's living in our walnut tree
Hasn't a clue about morality.
He seems to think it's perfectly all right
To pounce on little rodents in the night.
I tell him it's a cruel thing to do,
But all he answers is 'Tu-whit-tu-woo!'
Now if it were my lot to be an owl
I'd go and settle on the chimney-cowl
And if I saw a furry little mouse
Emerging from his subterranean house
I'd greet him with a friendly little hoot
And take to eating something else, like fruit.
The owl that's living in the walnut tree
Has little time for such a policy.
'We owls', he says, 'have grown accustomed to
'Demolishing a little mouse or two,'

And if I were to change my habit, why,
'My helpless little owlets all would die.
'Would that be such a moral thing to do?
'I hardly think it would. Tu-whit-tu-woo!
'Good Mr Darwin argued cogently
'Each species has its own morality.
'Under my moral code it's little mice
'Who nature says have got to pay the price.
'Were I to change my customary food
'I'd have to look for something else as good,
'And just suppose I took to eating you!
'What do you say to that? Tu-whit-tu-woo!'

THE FANTAIL

When walking in New Zealand you'll encounter now and then
A sort of cross between a fanlight window and a wren.
Along the forest path it hops about incessantly,
Keeping the woodland wayfarer in close proximity.
This pattern of behaviour, I will willingly confess,
It's tempting to interpret as a sign of friendliness,
And sentimental visitors who breathe the woodland air
May see themselves as partners in an avian love-affair.
I hesitate to rubbish this romantic point of view
But honesty obliges me to disillusion you.
It isn't that they love you, but they have a stratagem;
The midges follow you and so the fantail follows them.
If you dissect a fantail, as you take the bits apart,
You'll find the explanation in the stomach, not the heart.

So should you chance to walk among antipodean trees
And find yourself indulging in romantic fantasies,
By all means compliment the birds on what they have to do;
By eating up the midges they prevent them eating you!

FORTY WINKS

When Grandpa has his forty winks
It's more disturbing than he thinks,
And now that he's begun to snore
He's stepped it up to forty-four,
A most unwelcome increment
Of nothing less than ten percent.
The family is now in line
To cut it down to thirty-nine.

FRUITERER'S CHOICE

He sold it to us as the optimum
Incomparable dual-purpose plum,
But what he left discreetly undefined
Was what two purposes he had in mind.

GENETIC PAYBACK

'Twas I who gave you life, my lad,
And now you're in your teens!
My chromosomes you've always had
So may I have your jeans?

GRAVITY

Sir Isaac Newton, so the story goes,
Was snoozing underneath an apple tree.
An errant apple struck him on the nose
And, as they say, the rest is history.
Said he, 'I've just invented gravity;
'Now there's a thing to write a song about!
'Before my shattering discovery
'However did they get along without?
'Until that epoch-making circumstance
'Fruit must have hung for ever on the tree,
'So Eve, poor lady, never had the chance
'To manage with a windfall for her tea.
Had Newton been already on the scene
How different *that* story might have been!

HONEYED WORDS AND SUGARED SENTIMENTS

Honey is just a sugar of a rather special kind,
A product of the apiary, pure and unrefined.
A sugar-based economy is what supports the hive
And furnishes the wherewithal to keep the bees alive,
Within the bees' society their status and respect
Are measured by the quantity of honey they collect.
Unfortunately none of this is any use to me.
It's just my bleeding luck to be a diabetic bee.

THE HONORARY COLONEL

It happened many years ago. Sir Wingfield Worthington
Became a Lord Lieutenant, and a conscientious one.
There was an old tradition which expected him to be
The Honorary Colonel of a troop of cavalry.
Unfortunately nobody had told him that, of course,
For matters ceremonial he'd have to ride a horse.
This was a thing he never had attempted in his life.
It was, he thought, a hobby for his daughters and the wife.
But every time they held a ceremonial parade
He had to be on horseback to command the cavalcade.
Asserting his authority to issue a command,
He'd turn and face the troopers and the military band.
Anticipating trouble at his lack of horsemanship,
His officers suggested a mnemonetary tip –
When facing the procession from that elevated height,
Remember right is always 'left' and left is always 'right'.
He mentally repeated this ingenious little trick
Hoping that repetition would contrive to make it stick,
But rapidly discovered that this clever little ruse
Achieved the very opposite, to hopelessly confuse!
Arriving at the Market Place he turned his horse about
And magisterially tried to give the order out.
His thoughts were now in chaos, concentration in a blur;
'Parade will change direction left – no, right – no, as you were!'
The disrespectful public, unashamedly amused
To see this clumsy amateur distressingly confused,
Regarded his embarrassment with evident delight:
'Even a little four-year-old would know his left from right!'

The colonel, now convinced that he was going round the bend,
Made haste to bring these farcical proceedings to an end,
And in exasperation from his elevated seat
Roared out 'You bunch of idiots!   Get into Albert Street!'

HOSPITAL: THE MORNING AFTER

I should be thinking charitable things,
Doing my level best to empathise,
Trying to help him through his sufferings
And understand his agonising cries.
He doesn't know the trouble he has made
With his disruptive sleep-destroying tricks,
Roaring and barking like a cannonade
From half-past midnight until after six!
I should be eager to congratulate
Myself on being almost in command,
Still competent enough to demonstrate
My cool capacity to understand.
But if I've any surplus sympathy
I guess it's pretty well been spent on me!

IDENTITY CRISIS

'The English' Napoleon famously said,
'Are a nation of shopkeepers', so I have read.
But really, as Margaret Thatcher has taught us,
'We're more like a nation of shopkeepers' daughters!

JOHNNY FOREIGNER

Thank Heavens I'm an Englishman!
That's all I have to say.
The more I see of foreigners
The more I feel that way.
Why do we have to tolerate
Licentious Latin louts,
Mid-European layabouts
And lager-loaded Krauts?
Thank God I'm not an Itie or
An Arab or a Wog,
A garlic-reeking Dago or
A Francophonic Frog.
It's all these foreign languages
That plague a fellow so.
Why can't they stick to English? That's
What I should like to know.

It's good enough for Shakespeare and
For Churchill and for God;
It surely should be good enough
For any foreign sod.
The women on the Continent
Are either loose or tight;
Their menfolk drive like maniacs -
And on the bleeding right!
They've got no sense of humour and
They've got no sense of style.
Show 'em a decent job of work;
You'll see 'em run a mile!
'A mile' I said and meant it, and
I'm proud of it, so there!
This kilometric gibberish
Won't get us anywhere.
Thank God I'm free from prejudice!
Thank God I'm free from pride!
Self-righteousness and arrogance
I simply can't abide.
We English are a liberal
And open-minded lot;
We have a certain tolerance
The others haven't got.
Of course it gives us confidence
To know we're always right,
But why is Johnny Foreigner
So bloody impolite?

LANDSCAPE FROM THE SKY

Beautiful Boeing floating in the sky,
I mean to share your azimuthal eye
That lends a new dimension to the sight,
Revealing Earth from this Olympian height.
In you I find a new celestial ear

To catch the music of the stratosphere,
Where broken clouds can broken chords portray
As Galway's flute soars above Galway's Bay.
The sympathetic ear may clarify
The vision of the sympathetic eye;
So, fusing each contributory sense
In one celestial experience,
I'll not despise the gifts that science brings,
Press-studded symphonies and acid strings,
Their cutting edge like that great buoyant blade
Slicing thin clouds that nature left half-made,
As if to mock the laws of gravity
And find suspension where it shouldn't be.
As quilted landscapes, slowly vanishing
Beneath that huge obliterating wing,
Sneak slowly off at agonising pace
Miniscule islands burgeon in their place.
Even unwelcome cloudbanks swell sublime
As in the depths of geologic time,
And, though obscuring Earth's minutiae,
Inveigle, grasp and captivate the eye.
But clouds and skies and seas, however vast,
Are, like the rose, too beautiful to last.
Smart-suited girls, oozing authority,
Decree the blinds be drawn, and we comply.
The privilege these wings conferred on me
To share this God's-eye view of earth and sea
Is now withdrawn, for Hollywood today
Has come to meet its worshippers half-way.
The glory of the world must now depart;
Nature we love, but only after art.

Here in this silvered bird that cleaves the skies
Four hundred pairs of cabin-cloistered eyes,
Distracted from the true Divinity,
Turn to the idols of technology.
O neatly tailored stewardess, relent!
Grant one more glimpse from God's own firmament,
One furtive peep at Nova Scotia's plain,
The raw, defiant, tattered coast of Maine,
Secluded creeks where pilgrims worshipped God
Behind that sickle-shelter of Cape Cod.
Boston itself, from thirty thousand feet,
With puny tower and Lilliputian street,
Can open wide our self-deceiving eyes
And in an instant cut us down to size.
So what, I ask myself, on Judgment Day,
Will all these philistines presume to say,
Their eyes at last averted from the screen
Already buried in a magazine?
Hear me, your prophet, while there still is time
For you, like me, to savour the Sublime.
Revive that passion of the child to *see*,
Now moribund in adult apathy.
Sail on, majestic bird!   Sail through the skies
Till every pair of cabin-cloistered eyes
Acknowledges the gift which you have given
And sees Creation as it looks from Heaven!

LIT. CRIT.

A man we met in our hotel
Used the expression *'Bluh di Elle'*,
A phrase whose etymology
Was unfamiliar to me.
Now that I've had an hour or two
To settle down and think it through
I feel prepared to offer this
Extempore analysis:
We'll find the explanation in
Its Franco-German origin.

*

Consider, then, the German, *'Bluh'*.
Most probably it's new to you,
And I'll admit I'd never heard
This Palaeo-teutonic word,
Which, as you'll recognise, has now
Become, in modern German, *'Blau'*,
The colour of the summer skies,
Forget-me-nots and lovers' eyes,
But in this analytic game
It's recognisably the same.
So, trivialities apart,
We've made a pretty useful start.

*

The linking preposition, *'di'*
Needs no analysis from me.
The definition I would give
Is *'The Primeval Genitive'*.
In half a dozen forms or so,
Like *'di'* or *'de'* or *'da'* or *'do'*,
It's found in Latin countries, spread
Around the margins of the Med.

*

The meaning of the pronoun, *'Elle'*
Is not too difficult to tell.
In Gallic terminology
It signals femininity.
It doesn't matter what may be
Their status in society;
The Duchess and the common wench
Are equal targets for the French.
A manly chauvinistic male,

Downing his manly pint of ale,
Bearded, and idle to the bone
And bulging with testosterone,
Bearing a name like 'Mirabelle',
Would find us asking 'What the hell?'

*

So now we've reached the end of this,
My critical analysis,
And if you think it's balderdash
At least I've given it a bash.
Now see if you can do as well,
But say it quickly - *'Bluh-di-Elle!'*

MEDICAL JARGON

Confused about the terminology?
Well, here's an aid to jog your memory.
The definition of an '*-oscopy*'
Is what you have before an '*-ectomy*'!

A MORAL TALE RE-TOLD

The moral tale is often told
Of one who caught his death of cold
By venturing, the stupid prat,
On Ilkley Moor without a hat.
His grieving comrades had to lay
His body in the clammy clay
Where wiggly worms digested him,
(These moral tales are always grim!).
Luckily, though the man had died,
The story has a cheerful side.
A squadron of *Anatidae*,
('Ducks' to the likes of you and me),
Came nonchalantly sailing past
And ate the worms to break their fast.
Some of the mourners saw them there,
Fancied the ducks and grabbed a pair
And soon the contents of the grave
Were sizzling in the microwave.
The mourners served them, as one should,
With mushy peas and Yorkshire pud
And thus discovered in the end
That they had gobbled up their friend.
The moral message seems to be
About responsibility.
Though hardly in the best of taste,
It shows we *can* recycle waste!

MORNING TEA

Sheila was wondering if you'd be free
To come on Saturday for Morning Tea?

Kind of you, Bruce, but I've an allergy.
Unfortunately I react to tea,
So coffee is the beverage for me.
Could I have coffee, then, instead of tea?

No worries, Sunshine! Coffee it shall be,
But here we always *call* it 'Morning Tea'.

Well, 'Morning Coffee', for a Pom like me
Slips off the tongue a shade more easily.

In London, if you say so, that may be
But in Australia it's 'Morning Tea'.

You know it's coffee but you call it 'tea'?
What does that say about your honesty?

There speaks the English aristocracy!
Your haughty, spurious authority
Is only matched by your pomposity.
You seem to think we're still a colony!
We've got our individuality;
We've every right to call it 'Morning Tea'.

Yes, every right, but what keeps bugging me
Is this perverse irrationality.
If you served cyanide in A.C.T.
At ten a.m. you'd call it 'Morning Tea'!

I guess the time has come to change the tune.
Come for a beer tomorrow afternoon.

MY BUGGY

Guess what I've been and gone and done!
  I've bought a little toy.
It's shiny, red and lots of fun;
  Aren't I a lucky boy?

It's like a little motor car,
  This vehicle of mine;
It won't go fast, it won't go far
  But that just suits me fine.

Its horn, the cutest I have seen,
  Is pretty well unique;
It's like a sort of cross between
  A hiccup and a squeak.

So if you see a flash of red
  In Kingtree Avenue,
Prepare for choppy seas ahead
  And best of luck to you!

Perhaps you think four miles an hour
  Is much too slow to hurt.
Don't underestimate its power;
  You're all on red alert!

And if I should encounter you
  Walking the dog one day
I wouldn't recommend you to
  Contest my right of way!

You think I would capitulate?
  What would you like to bet?
Don't take too much for granted, mate,
  You ain't seen nothin' yet!

NORTH BAR, BEVERLEY, 1409-2009

Greetings to you who contemplate
This handsome medieval gate!
Relax a little while and spare
A thought for those who put it there.
Its function was for keeping out
People they weren't too sure about,
But now it serves for luring in
The visitors we want to win
So that we can with civic pride
Display the heritage inside.
Nothing now bars them from these sights
(Except, of course, the traffic lights),
Nor are we so particular
About what sort of folk they are;
We only have to make it clear
We want their money while they're here.
The architect would think it droll,
This strange reversal of its role,
But stranger still its legacy
For present-day technology.
For who, I wonder, would expect
A medieval architect,
With stunning perspicacity
Back in the fifteenth century,
To build a brick-built loading-gauge
To serve a traffic-conscious age
And thereby fix the guiding lines
For double-decker bus designs?

Unlikely as it may appear,
That actually happened here,
And medieval builders thus
Gave Beverley the Gothic Bus!

NU-SPEAK

We both speak English but it's not the same.
It's like you find me hard to comprehend.
I'm like 'My God'! A generation game?
I have to say, we get there in the end.
That's, to be honest, how it's always been.
It's what we use for punctuation. Right?
It's how we kind of speak. Know what I mean?
It isn't like we kind of have to fight.
I'm like - before I start to speak, you know,
I basically don't know what to say
Or how it basically ought to go.
Redundant words, like, slow it down. Okay?
So if you ask me what they're all about
It's like I kind of couldn't do without!

ON CHOOSING A SET OF TABLE MATS

Beware of that phenomenon,
The table mat with pictures on!
We've half a dozen sets of mats
From puppy dogs to pussy cats,
But each is prone to accident
With subsequent embarrassment.
There's one we like exceedingly,
'Australian ornithology'.
We used these mats the other day
When Auntie Kate had come to stay.
Concealed beneath her dinner plate,
Some ketchup, spilled by Auntie Kate,
Had landed in an awkward spot
And changed the picture quite a lot.
So when she moved her plate away
A little voice piped up to say
The sulphur-crested cockatoo
Had done a funny sort of poo,
A shrewd enough remark which led
To matters better left unsaid
And sadly failed to generate
A warm response in Auntie Kate.
While floral table mats are fine
To brighten up the way we dine,
Are not the animals and birds
Too unpredictable for words?
It's best to stick with common sense
And not go tempting Providence!

ON THE SQUEEZING OF DUCKS AND OTHER OBJECTS OF AFFECTION

('Ducksqueezer' has been recognised by lexicographers as a legitimate term for 'environmentalist').

If ever you should have the luck
To actually squeeze a duck,
To fondle, cuddle, hug and kiss -
What joy! What ecstasy! What bliss!
Indeed you even may forgive
My splitting an infinitive!
The verb 'to squeeze', I must confess,
Occasions some uneasiness.
Although such meanings as 'embrace'
I don't consider out of place,
Yet others in the O.E.D.
Seem less appropriate to me.

Expressions of a different sort,
Like 'crush' or 'crumple' or 'extort',
Are quite unsuited to express
Sympathy, love and tenderness.
And while I'm sure we all commend
Affection for our feathered friend
One wonders where it all will end.
A lapdog like the Pekinese
Thrives on a periodic squeeze,
And other pets around the house -
The cat, the hamster and the mouse -
Possess a pretty high degree
Of cuddly squeezability.
But if we fling the door too wide
And fail to stem the rising tide,
It won't be very long before
Endangered species by the score
Are lining up in expectation
Of sympathetic consolation,
Which, never mind how hard we try,
We simply cannot satisfy.
To squeeze a hippopotamus
Is patently ridiculous,
Yet conservationists agree
Its future is in jeopardy,
A dismal prospect which it shares
With elephants and polar bears;
So surely animals like these
Deserve a reassuring squeeze.
The only problem is their size;
They're just too big to pressurise.

Some animals, though small enough,
Are not composed of squeezy stuff;
So squeeze an oyster or a clam,
You'll find it doesn't give a damn,
While others you may wish to squeeze
Are far too slippery to seize;
The haddock and the conger eel,
Though well endowed with squeeze-appeal,
Need only give a single flip
To slither from the tightest grip.
But should your inclination lie
In squeezing, say, a butterfly,
Your misdirected tenderness
Could make a pretty nasty mess.
While other animals than these
May like the comfort of a squeeze
And may be thought to qualify,
It's inadvisable to try.
'Now Wilbur, dear, for heaven's sake
'Go easy on that rattlesnake!
'I really doubt he likes to be
'Embraced with such ferocity'.
There's a thin line of separation
Between a squeeze and strangulation.
Somewhere one has to draw the line,
Not least in matters serpentine;
A python in the living-room
Prompts one to ask 'Who squeezes whom?'

*

Once, when I was a little boy,
A duckling was my favourite toy,
And when I squeezed its rubber back
It made a semblance of a quack.
But now I've more than had enough
Of all this sentimental stuff,
So I should like my duckling, please,
With orange sauce, French fries and peas,
And let my guts apply the squeeze!

OPERA

Opera, sir, is just a waste of time!
Singing's not *natural*, and, just as bad,
If all our conversation were in rhyme
People would think we'd all gone barking mad!
The culmination of absurdity
Has surely got to be the moment where
The tenor sings in perfect harmony
With folk he's not supposed to know are there!
This world of operatic fantasy
Doesn't impress me, not one little bit!
It's out of contact with reality.
Only a halfwit could believe in it!

But what's the use of arguing all night?
People like you will never see the light!

PARLEZ-VOUS FRANGLAIS?

A patriotic sentiment
Impelled young François to resent
How English idioms entrench
Themselves among the native French.
He simply couldn't come to grips
With phrases like *'le fish-and-chips'*!
An outright ban he thought would seem
Unnecessarily extreme
And yet he simply couldn't bear
These English insults everywhere.
A trouble-shooter, if he's wise,
Will try and find a compromise,
And that's how François found a way
To keep the enemy at bay.
New English words he *can* abide
But only if they're Frenchified,
So, since he thought of it last week,
We now have *'le computerspique'*!

PARLIAMENTARY CANDIDATE

The cricketer, Tom Ballantine,
Is now the Party's choice.
He's sure to urge the party line
With a persuasive voice.
One weapon in his armoury
Is bound to help him win:
A leg-break bowler's got to be
A connoisseur of spin.

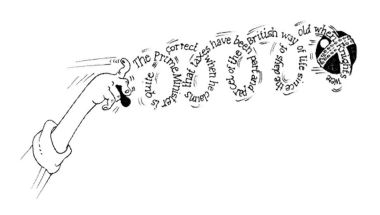

PICASSO

Painters conspiring in a plot
To make things seem what they are not
Will likely find their work to be
A test of credibility.
With eyes and noses changing place
A re-constructed human face
Seems to a philistine like me
A pointless waste of energy.
Let those who will employ their wits
Moving around the various bits,
But leave old-fashioned folk like me
To leave them where they used to be.

PICKING ON PRESCOTT

When Prescott was required to steer the ship,
(Blair being absent on a foreign trip),
A hostile and unsympathetic press,
Spurred on by malice and vindictiveness,
Seized on a croquet game to represent
His irresponsible mismanagement.
History tells us, many years ago,
About a game of bowls on Plymouth Hoe.
The Spanish sailors, spoiling for a fight,
Against the Brits, already were in sight

When Francis Drake achieved immortal fame
By obstinately finishing his game.
Hailed as a national celebrity,
His *sangfroid* earned him immortality,
So why should Prescott's harmless croquet game
Not earn him too an honourable name?
Though croquet is a vicious game to play
No-one can labour all the livelong day.
We all need time for some relaxing sport;
Some choose the golf course, some the tennis court.
Those who would think the croquet lawn amiss
Must clearly share the press's prejudice.
Is it that croquet is supposed to be
The birthright of the aristocracy
And thus indecent for a working man
To spend a little time on when he can?
That's Prescott's business; let us mind our own
And leave this honourable man alone!

THE POET

To make a poet, people seem to think,
There has to be some eccentricity
Driving the hapless victim to the brink
Of madness, folly, crime or tragedy.
A miserable childhood is a start,
A crippling illness, an unbalanced mind,
An unrequited passion of the heart
Or all of these calamities combined.
Is this the secret of proficiency?
Is this the talisman to bring success?
Is this the passport to celebrity,
The mark of literary worthiness?
Must the poor poet suffer all this crap?
Can't he just be an ordinary chap?

PRESS ONE

Give me a Ruth, a Susie or a Joyce,
Or even, if you must, some nameless bloke
To greet me with a warm, responsive voice,
Leavening business with a friendly joke.
This pre-recorded anonymity,
('Press one, press two, press three or even four'),
Can drive a fellow to insanity.
I don't think I can take it any more!
I somehow feel a chap can never win
This game of patience-via-technology.
There's precious little sign of *culture* in
A world devoid of personality.
Technology's rewards, however nice,
Come at a pretty formidable price!

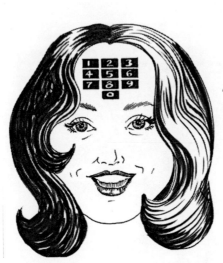

"HELLO –
MY NAME'S RUTH.
THERE WAS AN
ENGLISHMAN,
AN IRISHMAN AND
A SCOTSMAN . . ."

PRICES SLASHED

The little supermarket in our town
Sets out its prices in a novel way,
Stressing how much the price is coming down
Rather than saying what we have to pay.
So we have BOGOF, (buy one get one free),
Save 20p on Mr Kipling's cakes,
Fifty percent reduction on our tea,
Amazing offers on our T-bone steaks.
These price concessions by the management
Reflect a user-friendly policy,
A philanthropic, generous intent
Earning a rightful popularity.
'Not bloody likely!' says the customer,
'It merely shows how over-priced they were!'

SMASHING THAT GRECIAN URN

Beauty is truth, truth beauty - that is all
It takes to drive a fellow up the wall!
If Mr Keats had stopped to think it out
He must have felt an element of doubt.
Had he made time to study either word
He would have known the saying is absurd.
It didn't seem to worry him a bit
As long as he could get away with it.
Truth surely means the opposite of lies -
Not having any truck with 'porky-pies'.
Whatever beauty is, it's evident
It's got to be entirely different.
Look at the beauty parlour. I believe
It only has one function, to deceive.
Its very purpose surely has to be
Rooted and grounded in mendacity.
Tarting-up middle age to look like youth?
For God's sake, what has that to do with truth?
At last we have exposed his little game,
Trying to make it out they're both the same!
Yes, Mr Keats, we've got you on the run.
Do us a favour. Pull the other one!

THE SORCERER'S APPRENTICE

Before we even think about a plan
To make dictatorships democracies,
Invading Syria, threatening Iran,
We need to face the practicalities.
The best intentions are of no avail
Unless they pass the culminating test.
The Sorcerer's Apprentice is a tale
That all our politicians should digest.
In flat defiance of authority
The brash apprentice, left to mind the shop,
Sets off a mindless piece of sorcery,
Not understanding how to make it stop.
Walt Disney scored a memorable goal,
Giving a gormless mouse the title role!

TALK OF THE DEVIL

Just when I chucked him out it's hard to say,
But yes, I sent Beelzebub away,
Got rid of him with his satanic tricks
Probably round about the age of six.
With Father Christmas and the Fairy Queen
I found I didn't need him on the scene.
Abstract ideas we take, and if we please
We turn them into personalities.
Buildings and places also we contrive
To treat as if they really were alive.
The Kremlin's broadside, aimed at Washington,
Raised the blood-pressure of the Pentagon.
The Oval Office made the feathers fly
But wisely chose to keep its powder dry.

Brussels in turn replied predictably
By blowing Uncle Sam a raspberry.
When Wall Street made an unprovoked attack
The Bank of England stabbed it in the back.
Number Eleven scored a winner when
It took the Mickey out of Number Ten.
The Quai d'Orsay was furious of course,
The Vatican expressed its deep remorse,
Meanwhile an inattentive Scotland Yard
Was carelessly hoist with its own petard.
Things which we know to be inanimate
We casually make articulate.
Although it is deceptive in a way,
It's nothing new. We do it every day.
Talk of the Devil, then, is just a lot
Of idle, superstitious Tommy Rot.
He's a fictitious figure we invent
To make unruly miscreants repent.
If Tel Aviv and Cairo come to blows,
Leaving each other with a bloody nose,
How will it end? The Devil only knows!

THREE WISHES

When Mister Henry Palliser
  Was walking by the sea
He met a fairy visitor
  Quite unexpectedly,
And, being rather struck with her,
  Invited her to tea.

She came a week or two ago,
  Armed with her *Fairy News*,
Which had an offer on the go
  That he could not refuse:
'Three wishes for their readers!', so
  What would he like to choose?

For Number One he went for health,
  Freedom from malady.
For Number Two he fancied wealth;
  Good-bye to poverty!
Then with imaginative stealth
  He pondered Number Three.

To no-one in the Nursery Rhymes
  That he had ever heard,
Not even in the Pantomimes,
  Had this idea occurred;
He thought it over several times
  And then he chose the Third.

'Two of my wishes now have gone;
  'I've made my choice', said he.
'Now comes the true criterion
  'Of ingenuity.
'This is the wish I've settled on:
  'I'll take another three!'

Nobody ever thought of that
  Until he came along.
The game that he was playing at
  Seemed to be going strong,
And if the fairy smelt a rat
  Let's hope she'd got it wrong!

The chance to halt this strategy
  She realised had gone.
Palliser's opportunity
  Could now go on and on.
For story-tellers this would be
  A new phenomenon.

Responding to her offer he
  Had now produced his ace.
The damage to her dignity
  Was more than she could face.
Her well-intentioned charity
  Was ending in disgrace.

Said she 'This fellow is a pain;
  'He's made a fool of me.
'He's found a way to start again
  'Each time he gets to three,
'Heading with all his might and main
  'Towards infinity!

'He'll ask for whisky and champagne
  'In perpetuity,
'And every time he's bound to gain
  'More credibility.
'What can I think of to regain
  'My lost authority?'

She went to see a barrister
   Proficient in the law,
(Which filled the anxious Palliser
   With apprehensive awe),
To see if he could find for her
   Some legalistic flaw.

Said he 'No need to find a cure!
   'At such a song and dance
'No judge in the Judicature
   'Would give a second glance.
'Without your legal signature
   'He hasn't got a chance!'

The grateful fairy, welcoming
   This promising advice,
Now set her mind on punishing
   Palliser's avarice
And publicly disparaging
   Greed as a shameful vice.

She went away elated, and
   On an impulsive whim
Took instant flight to Fairyland
   As in the Brothers Grimm,
And, brandishing her fairy wand,
   Eliminated him!

TWELVE P.M.

I'm horrified to find the BBC
Employing the expression 12 PM,
A pair of letters which undoubtedly
Stands for the Latin *post meridiem*,
The hour of twelve, it stands to common sense,
Denotes an actual moment of the day.
The *'after*-noon' can clearly not commence
Until the hour of twelve has passed away.
The BBC, as every schoolboy knows,
Should be the guardian of our English tongue.
Whether we write in poetry or prose
This blatant inconsistency is wrong.
So, BBC, I leave you with a quiz:
'How can the time be later than it is?'[1]

---

[1] (The BBC has now seen the light; it's 12 noon or 12 midnight!)

0°
Longitude

Here Endeth
ye Morning

Here Beginneth
ye Afternoon

RIVER THAMES

GREENWICH

Here
lies
NOON
who
passed away
too soon

80

THE VANGUARD

(Addressed to General Sir Brian Robertson
on his appointment to run British Railways)

To any military man
How strange it must appear
That, though the guard be in the van,
The van is in the rear!

with acknowledgements
to ROLAND EMETT

WALT WHITMAN

"The aria sinking,
All else continuing, the stars shining,
The winds blowing, the notes of
the bird continuous echoing..."

I used to think it must have been
  A cruel turn of fate
That placed me in this earthly scene
  A century too late.

Poets had built a heritage
  By writing rhyming verse.
In that iconoclastic age
  They changed it for the worse.

Whitman, the author of the crime,
  With whom the rot began,
Famously said 'Thou shalt not rhyme
  'And neither shalt thou scan!'

So then, with all the rules relaxed,
  The laws of prosody
Were systematically axed
  And all was anarchy.

'But is it fair' I hear you say,
  'To blame it all on Walt?
'Cos in a funny sort of way
  'It's everybody's fault.'

For if it isn't poetry
  And if it isn't prose,
What is its true identity?
  The devil only knows.

We need to find another name
  For this perversity
And not let Whitman take the blame
  In perpetuity.

The outlook, though, is not so grim;
  The prospect could be worse.
We don't all have to follow him
  And write that kind of verse.

So here's my gesture of dissent.
  This simple doggerel
Informs you of my sentiment
  (And rhymes and scans as well!).

EPILOGUE

When Franz Schubert died they gathered together some of his unpublished songs and made them into a song-cycle to which they gave the name *Schwanengesang*, Swansong. The allusion is to an ancient myth, that, before it dies, a swan, for the first and only time, bursts into song.

A more up-to-date if less romantic version of the story says: 'It isn't over till the Fat Lady sings'. Well, in my ninetieth year I can already hear the Fat Lady doing her breathing exercises and warming up with a few *coloratura arpeggios* offstage. I therefore thought it time to gather up some poetic bits and pieces so as to give the Fat Lady something to sing about.

Jay Appleton,
Cottingham,
East Yorkshire.
2009.

Lightning Source UK Ltd.
Milton Keynes UK
23 November 2009

146631UK00001B/15/P